Live Music

By Ron Berman

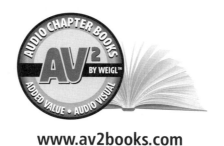

www.av2books.com

Your AV² Media Enhanced book gives you an online audio book, and a self-assessment activity. Log on to www.av2books.com and enter the unique book code from this page to access these special features.

Go to **www.av2books.com**, and enter this book's unique code.

BOOK CODE

M283639

AV² by Weigl brings you media enhanced books that support active learning.

AV² Audio Chapter Book Navigation

HIGHLIGHTED TEXT   ACTIVITIES   HOME   CLOSE

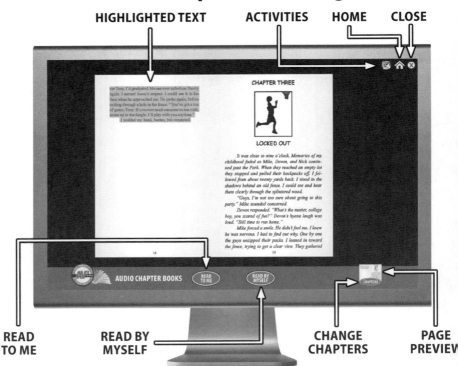

READ TO ME

READ BY MYSELF

CHANGE CHAPTERS

PAGE PREVIEW

Published by AV² by Weigl
350 5ᵗʰ Avenue, 59ᵗʰ Floor
New York, NY 10118

Website: www.av2books.com   www.weigl.com

First Published by Scobre Educational Press.

Library of Congress Control Number: 2013937468
ISBN 978-1-62127-984-6 (hardcover)
ISBN 978-1-62127-940-2 (single-user eBook)
ISBN 978-1-48960-015-8 (multi-user eBook)

Printed in the United States of America in North Mankato, Minnesota
1 2 3 4 5 6 7 8 9 0 17 16 15 14 13

062013
WEP310513

2

TABLE OF CONTENTS

Live

Music

Chapter One

The Broken Heart Brigade

All across the United States, something exciting is happening. Teenagers are picking up guitars and pounding away on drum sets. These young musicians are creating the music of tomorrow.

A great example of this is The Broken Heart Brigade. They are a band from Diamond, Ohio. This small town is about 50 miles away from Cleveland. The band is together almost every day. They play music, work on new songs, and try to improve their skills. Like thousands of other bands, they want to make it in the music business.

On this chilly fall afternoon, the band is getting ready to rehearse. Brandi adjusts the high hats on her drum set. Meanwhile, Ozzie and Zach tune their guitars. Isaac is also busy. He carefully ties a bandana around his head. He often wears one when the band practices, and sometimes when they perform.

As they start playing, Ozzie steps up to the mic. His powerful voice is sharp and clear. It's obvious that he has been influenced by many other bands. One of these bands is My Chemical Romance. Most of their fans love their classic song "Welcome to the Black Parade." When their fans hear the first line, they recognize the unique voice of Gerard Way.

Being compared to someone as talented as Gerard Way makes Ozzie proud. After all, he's a huge fan of My Chemical Romance. If they heard Ozzie sing, they would probably become fans of his as well.

Ozzie

18-year-old Ozzie Thomas is a normal teenager with many interests. He goes to church, and loves *Star Wars* and Tim Burton movies. When it comes to music, he listens to many different bands. There's much more to Ozzie, though. He also sings and plays guitar for The Broken Heart Brigade.

Before music came into Ozzie's life, it was all about sports. He has played basketball and baseball for as long as he can remember. He would still be pitching today if he hadn't suffered a shoulder injury. After his baseball injury, he focused more on basketball.

At six-foot-two, Ozzie is the starting center of the Southeast High Pirates. Of course, his schedule is busier than most athletes. He goes to basketball practice, lifts weights, and plays league games. He also spends just as much time practicing with his band.

According to Ozzie, his music career started when he was 14 years old. His dad decided to take the family shopping— at Guitar Center. When Mr. Thomas was a kid, he and his brother had played music together. Now it was Ozzie's turn to play with *his* younger brother, Isaac. By the time the family returned home, Ozzie had a beautiful new guitar. And he's been playing it ever since.

The Broken Heart Brigade begins practice by playing some covers. A "cover" is when a band performs a song that was recorded by a different musician. An hour later, they're still at it. Band practice is completely different from sports practice. Here, there is no coach yelling out instructions. The mood is very relaxed—even goofy at times.

At the moment, Ozzie, Brandi, and Isaac are laughing as Zach describes every detail of the hernia surgery he just had. He reaches into his guitar case for a brown envelope: "Check out these pics my surgeon gave me after the operation."

8

"No thanks," Isaac says, pretending to be disgusted. "Dude, nobody else would carry around pictures of the blood and guts inside his body!"

Zach grins and walks over to Brandi, photos in hand. She's trying not to crack up with laughter. She holds up her hand like a police officer stopping traffic. "Don't even THINK about it, Zach."

All four of them are laughing, but what Isaac said is true. What's also true is that Zach is a unique teenager. He's interested in things that many of his friends wouldn't even understand.

Zach

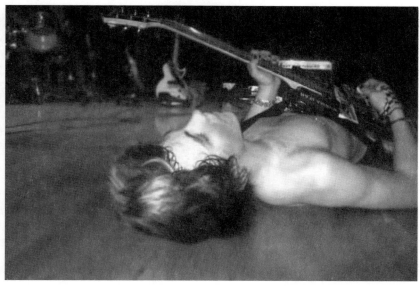

In addition to music, 18-year-old Zach Kuntz has always had many other hobbies. He has enjoyed riding four-wheelers and being on the wrestling team. He has also run track and taken piano. Another one of his interests is the human body.

"I've always been fascinated by how the body works," Zach explains. "It's cool how we can help it heal from wounds or diseases. We now have the opportunity to live longer and better than ever before."

Bones, muscles, joints, organs—these are just some of the basics of the human body. It's important to learn about these things. For example, some college students are studying to become doctors. Understanding the human body will make them better doctors in the future.

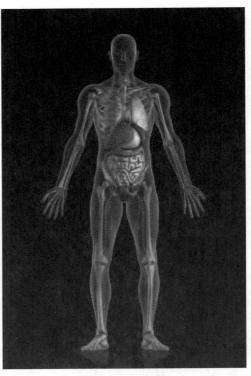

Obviously, Zach isn't grossed out by the blood and guts inside his body. He even asked the doctor to take pictures during his hernia surgery! Zach appreciates these types of things. One day he may become a doctor or do medical research. These are good career choices. Sure, they're not as exciting as being a rock star. But they help make the world a better place.

After the laughter over the photos dies down, things begin to get serious. The band decides to work on a new song Ozzie has written. As the chorus kicks in, Brandi leads the way with her powerful drumming. People always say how cool it is that she's the only girl in a band with three other guys. It's never been a big deal to her, though.

"I have a brother who is seven years older than me. I also have a bunch of cousins who are boys, so I'm used to it," *she explains.*

Isaac nods his head in agreement. He adds, "We're always messing around and picking on each other. Brandi's just like one of the guys. If any of us messes with her, she always dishes it right back."

Brandi

"That was the night I fell in love with music."

Brandi Walden is talking about the first concert she ever attended. She was just ten years old. Her family took her to see the bands Poison and Cinderella. Both of these bands were popular in the 1980s and '90s.

Brandi will never forget that show. When Poison did their famous song "Every Rose Has Its Thorn," the crowd went wild. The drummers had a huge impact on Brandi. She wanted to be like them—up there on the stage, drumsticks in hand.

After that concert, Brandi began playing percussion in band class. At the time, she was in the fifth grade. She played the snare drum, bells, and other percussion instruments.

Things really started happening by the time Brandi was in the eighth grade. It was 2005, and 14-year-old Brandi was beginning to show some real skill on the drums. When Christmas rolled around, she received her very own drum kit. "It was the happiest day of my life," she recalls.

A deep love of music runs in Brandi's family. Her father, Jack Walden, is the manager of The Broken Heart Brigade. Her uncle, Nik, is a great musician. In fact, the first time Brandi ever played live was with her uncle.

Brandi, only 15 years old at the time, was very nervous. They were at a cool little club called David B's. It was packed. Brandi tried to appear calm. Inside, though, she was scared.

Rocking out: Brandi and her uncle.

Brandi and her uncle's band performed Led Zeppelin's classic song "Rock and Roll." Brandi did an excellent job and the crowd cheered loudly. This amazing experience helped motivate her to become a great drummer.

As the band practices Ozzie's song, Isaac feels that something is missing. All of a sudden, an idea hits him. He looks over at his older brother. "Hey Ozzie, what if you replace the second line with the first line? And also change the words 'hey girl' to 'see the world'. I'll bet that will make the chorus flow better."

Right away, Ozzie and Zach understand what he's talking about. "Yeah, Isaac, good call. C'mon, let's try it."

After only one take with the new lyrics, everyone is telling Isaac that he's a genius! Just like that, the chorus sounds more natural. And it makes the song much better. No one else in the band could have figured that out. They don't look at things the way Isaac does. Actually, very few people look at things the way he does.

Isaac

Isaac Thomas has always had a creative mind. The other members of The Broken Heart Brigade think he writes great lyrics. This is a skill that has always come easily to him. Growing up, his big brother Ozzie would usually be playing the guitar. Meanwhile, Isaac would be in his room, writing or reading.

15-year-old Isaac is very popular and has lots of friends. However, he doesn't always follow the crowd. Instead, Isaac chooses to be himself—even in situations where other people might judge him.

A perfect example of this is the Silver Ring Thing. This is a program that Isaac participates in. It helps teenagers to remain sexually abstinent until marriage. Being sexually "abstinent" means not having sex. Many people would laugh at this, but not Isaac. He is a good role model for other teenagers.

Isaac's brave choice is shared by another group of musicians. They are much different from the pop punk and emo hardcore styles he loves. Still, Isaac admits he has respect for the Jonas Brothers. They are famous for their "purity rings." Like Isaac, they have remained true to what they believe. This isn't always easy. They've been the butt of jokes on the Internet and on TV.

Isaac knows that many important people in history have been laughed at. He also knows that it didn't stop them. Both the Jonas Brothers and Isaac Thomas should be applauded. They have the courage to stand up for what they believe.

Four hours later, The Broken Heart Brigade finally stops practicing. By now they're wiped out. They all feel satisfied after a very good afternoon. They had planned to rehearse for an hour or two. Once they started, they didn't want to stop playing. This happens to them a lot. It's because they love playing together.

For The Broken Heart Brigade, and for bands all around the world, it's all about the music.

Chapter Two

It's All About the Music

It's normal to hear loud music coming from Brandi Walden's home in Diamond, Ohio. The neighbors know it's not coming from the radio, or even Zach's iPod. It's The Broken Heart Brigade, playing downstairs in the basement.

It's Zach on his Billie Joe Armstrong Signature Guitar. It's Ozzie on his Schecter Synyster guitar—named for Avenged Sevenfold's lead guitarist, Synyster Gates. And it's Isaac and Brandi, in sync as always, on bass and drums.

Drums, bass, two guitars, and a lead singer. This has

been the lineup of many great bands. It was the lineup for one of the most famous bands ever, the Beatles. And even modern bands like The Killers and Foo Fighters use this same lineup.

Music is exciting because there are no rules. A band doesn't *have* to have two guitar players. Just look at Jack and Meg White. They formed a two-person band and called themselves the White Stripes. Their unique style made them famous.

The Broken Heart Brigade is doing the same thing. Day after day, these four teenagers can be found downstairs in Brandi's basement. They're developing *their own* style. It's all about rocking out, being with friends, and having fun playing music.

That's the way it should be. Sure, Diamond, Ohio, isn't Hollywood or New York. It's a long distance from where bands like U2 or Green Day record their albums. But that's what makes music so awesome. No matter where you are, you can still enjoy it. Music is a wild ride and anyone can feel the rush.

Teenagers understand this better than anyone. Music is fun, and music is natural. It has a huge influence on the world. Not everyone is a talented musician. But anyone can participate simply by listening. It's not just about rocking out in a band—it's about how music makes all of us *feel*.

There's music, and then there's the music *business*. These are not the same things. Think about a person who learns how to play guitar today. He or she is no different from someone who learned guitar fifty years ago. The music business, on the other hand, has definitely changed.

Years ago, there were tons of great bands you didn't even know about. Unless you lived in the same town, how would you have heard of them? Luckily, the Internet and digital music has changed all of this.

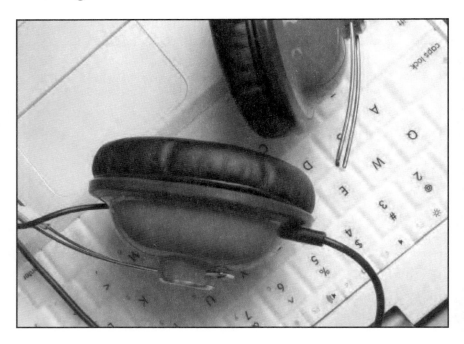

Technology has made everything easier. It certainly has for The Broken Heart Brigade. The band has a cool MySpace page. More than 20,000 people have checked it out. On their MySpace page, you can hear their songs "On My Own" and "Love Like Lemonade."

One day, hopefully this promising young band will hit it big. If so, you can say you knew about them before a lot of other people. You can say that you were a fan of "On My Own" from the very beginning.

Before the Internet, the radio was the easiest way to find out about new songs and bands. Songs that came on the radio quite often became hits. Young people would then go to record stores and buy the album. Radio also played a big part in drawing people to live shows.

Some music fans would also read magazines like *Rolling Stone*, *Billboard*, or *Spin*. This was another way to keep up with the music scene. And then there was the album itself. Albums contained information such as lyrics, photos, and artwork. If you were a music fan during the 1950s and '60s, you were probably listening to vinyl. These round, 12-inch records were played on a record player.

By the 1970s, cassette tapes had become the new way of listening to music. Cassettes were eventually passed by CDs in the early 1990s. Of course, we all know what has passed CDs— MP3s. Who knows if  some new technology will come along soon. Maybe it will make even MP3s seem old-fashioned.

Through the years, TV has also been very important for music fans. A weekly show called *American Bandstand* began in the 1950s. It featured musical performances, dancing, and a live studio audience. *American Bandstand* was an extremely popular show for many years.

Another important show was *Soul Train*. It focused mainly on African-American artists. *Soul Train* was all about music, fashion, and dance. Many superstars have appeared on this show. They have included Ludacris, Mariah Carey, Paula Abdul, Black Eyed Peas, and Queen Latifah.

In the 1980s, a new form of TV began—MTV. It started out as a 24-hour music video channel. Suddenly, people could *see* their favorite singers and bands on TV. It was a great way to discover new music. MTV helped many artists and bands become popular.

TV and radio have always had a huge impact on music. Still, nothing even comes close to the Internet. Once music went digital—and online—it was a whole new world. Nothing would ever be the same again.

At first, the Internet seemed bad for the music business. During the late 1990s, file sharing became popular. Some people might remember the original Napster. It was the first big file-sharing program. All it took were simple clicks of your mouse. Just like that, you could quickly download songs onto your computer—for free. Naturally, record companies were not very pleased! They didn't want people to get music without paying for it.

These problems aren't as serious anymore. Sure, illegal downloading still takes place. But now you can find easy and cheap downloads on iTunes and other websites. So there's not as much of a reason to steal music. In addition, there are websites such as MySpace Music. They allow listeners to stream music or download some songs for free.

These days, there are so many new bands for music fans to discover. It's not only about what's happening in your city or town anymore. Now, day or night, you can hear or see all kinds of music. Because of the Internet, you can even communicate with your favorite band.

There's nothing like being at a live show.

Not everything has changed, though. Musicians still have the same dreams they've always had. They still want to get a deal with a record company. They want to perform in front of thousands of people. And of course, most musicians want to be rich and famous.

For bands like The Broken Heart Brigade, these are exciting times. They already have fans in Ohio. Being on MySpace has also opened some other doors for them. They've talked to people all across the country. They were even contacted by a record company in London, England.

Long way from London, England: Even from snowy Ohio, bands like The Broken Heart Brigade are making the type of music that record companies are looking for.

The Broken Heart Brigade has also been emailing with a record company in California. Having a MySpace page is very helpful for the band. It means that the company in California can listen to their songs. They can also see photos of the band.

The members of The Broken Heart Brigade realize that anything is possible. Their careers are just starting to take off. It is very impressive. After all, they only formed their band a couple of years ago. In the beginning, they had no idea what was going to happen.

"The four of us starting a band must have been a really awesome coincidence," Isaac says.

"I think it's more than that," replies Brandi. "It couldn't have just been a coincidence."

"Destiny?" Zach offers.

"Either way," Ozzie smiles, "it's all about the music."

** DID YOU KNOW? ** The first video ever shown on MTV was "Video Killed the Radio Star." It was a song by a group called The Buggles. The video sure looks different from videos of today.

Chapter Three

Childhood Friends

Diamond, Ohio, is a very small town of less than 3,000 people. Four of these people are Ozzie Thomas, his brother Isaac, Zach Kuntz, and Brandi Walden. They were all childhood friends.

"We just liked hanging out together," Zach remembers. "Growing up, we would have pool parties at Ozzie and Isaac's house. Sometimes we would go to the movies or bowling or something. No matter what, it was always the four of us."

Above: Brandi and Ozzie. Below: Isaac and Zach.

There have been other bands whose members were also childhood friends. A kid named Mike Dirnt comes to mind. He grew up in California near his buddy, Billie Joe. They formed a band when they were 14 years old, naming it Sweet Children. The name didn't stick, though. They changed it to a name most music fans know very well—Green Day.

Growing up, the four friends all followed their own interests. For Brandi, it was always music. Seeing Poison and Cinderella perform live when she was ten years old changed her life. She continued to go to concerts. In May of 2005, she took Ozzie and another friend to a live show. On the bill was one of Brandi's favorite bands, Simple Plan. Good Charlotte and Reliant K were also playing.

For Ozzie, the concert was an eye-opener. The lead singers were amazing. So were the guitar players. By this time, Ozzie had been playing guitar for a couple of years. Still, he was more of a jock than a musician. After that night, however, everything changed. He decided that he wanted to get more involved with music.

Six months later, another important musical event took place. It was November of 2005. Brandi had two tickets to the House of Blues in Cleveland. Simple Plan, Paramore, and Plain White T's were playing. At first Ozzie wanted to go, but he had a basketball game that night. So Brandi invited Isaac, who jumped at the chance to see his first live show. He was fired up because one of his favorite bands was playing. "Brandi loves Simple Plan, but I really wanted to see Paramore," Isaac says.

The concert was fantastic. Isaac was totally blown away. Going to his first live show inspired him to become a serious musician.

By then, Ozzie had become an excellent guitar player. Isaac figured he would take after his brother. "It didn't quite work out that way," he laughs. "I played guitar, but *very* badly." Isaac didn't know it at the time, but there was a reason for it. Guitar was not meant to be his instrument.

Brandi, Ozzie, and Isaac grab a bite to eat before heading to a concert.

Around that same time, Isaac started getting into the band Fall Out Boy. He spent hours listening to their hit album *From Under the Cork Tree*. He loved their music video for "Sugar, We're Goin' Down." As a matter of fact, it helped him find his true calling. "I was so inspired by Pete Wentz, that I switched to bass," Isaac explains. Once he did, everything fell into place for him as a musician.

Fall Out Boy was a major influence not only on Isaac, but the entire band. The style of The Broken Heart Brigade can be described as "pop punk." This is a type of music that is performed by bands like Yellowcard, Good Charlotte, and many others. It's a high-energy, exciting style of music.

Pop punk started back in the 1970s. Bands like the Ramones made a new type of rock and roll popular. It was known back then as punk rock. Their music was all about simple, speedy songs. They used nothing more than voice, guitar, bass, and drums.

Punk rock had a lot of fans during the 1980s and early 1990s. Still, it was not as popular as other forms of rock and roll. Musically, that time period will mostly be remembered for glam and grunge. Glam was as much about the fashion as the music. It was guys with big hair, decked out in crazy clothes. Some of them wore tons of makeup on their faces.

As for grunge, most people immediately think about the band Nirvana. Their second album, *Nevermind*, is considered one of the greatest albums of the 1990s. Some people described grunge as a cross between punk and metal. It was basically a raw rock sound. It had a lot of crunching guitars and huge drums.

In 1994, music changed once again. Green Day released their album, *Dookie*. It brought the band huge success, and made punk rock popular again. By now it was usually called pop punk. During the rest of the '90s, many other pop punk bands came on the scene. These included The Offspring, Bad Religion, and Bink-182.

With the turn of the century, pop punk remained popular. Bands such as Sum 41 and Good Charlotte released hit singles. Meanwhile, Green Day and Blink-182 were also very busy. In 2002, they headlined the Pop Disaster Tour. Since that time, pop punk has continued to be an important part of the music scene.

As for Zach, he was the last one to join his friends in becoming a musician. He saw how much fun everyone was having learning an instrument. So in the spring of 2006, Zach did the same thing. Following Ozzie's lead, he chose guitar. He quickly fell in love with the instrument. "I bought my first guitar for $75," Zach remembers. "It was a Fender Squier that I got from a friend of mine. I started playing it day and night."

Zach's situation is interesting because he didn't take any lessons. Instead, he learned basic chords from a tab book. Plus, Ozzie would come over and show him different things. "I just kept practicing and picking up on stuff," Zach says. With that kind of dedication, it's no wonder he improved so quickly.

By that summer, Ozzie, Brandi, and Isaac had also improved a great deal. They were all developing their own musical styles. Still, the four friends weren't talking about forming a band. Luckily, though, they had taken up different instruments.

"We didn't plan it that way," Brandi says. "That's why we say it was destiny. I mean, I ended up on drums. Isaac fell in love with bass. Ozzie and Zach became awesome guitar players. How cool is that?"

This was an important time for these friends. The timing wasn't quite right for them to become a band. That would soon change. Within six months they would be starting an incredible musical journey together.

** DID YOU KNOW? ** The band Paramore shares something in common with The Broken Heart Brigade. Their four members are also from a small town— Franklin, Tennessee. It has a population of 55,000. Sure, that's bigger than Diamond, Ohio. Still, it's tiny compared to the cities where Paramore now performs (such as Los Angeles, with a population of more than 9 million).

Chapter Four

Rock School

During summer vacation in 2006, Brandi signed up for "Rock School" at a music store. To help explain Rock School, think back to the movie *School of Rock*. In the movie, Jack Black plays a substitute teacher. He uses music as a way of bringing students together. By the time it's over, he has turned them into a tight band.

Brandi mentioned her summer plans to Ozzie, Zach, and Isaac. They were still practicing instruments on their own. None of them showed much interest in joining her at Rock School. They may have felt that it would be a waste of time. Or maybe they didn't have the confidence just yet.

Rock School was six weeks long. Groups of four students were placed with one instructor. Together, they would learn about playing live and giving a good performance.

The end of Rock School would take place at an auditorium called Kent Stage. Each "band" would perform a couple of songs. The pressure would be on, since families were invited to watch.

When the final night of Rock School arrived, Brandi felt ready. By then she had already gained a little bit of live experience. She had played with her uncle at the club. So although she was nervous, she was also excited. It ended up being a very successful night. Brandi and her bandmates were even in the newspaper!

Rock rookie

It's a six-week and rocky road for teen music hopefuls

By Malcolm X Abram
Beacon Journal staff writer

You've seen School of Rock, the comedic film in which a wannabe rock star poses as a substitute teacher and tries to turn his class into a rock band.

There's no Jack Black at Woodsy's Music in Kent, but there is Rock School – a six-week program where teenage wannabe rock stars get to learn from music teachers how to become a rock band.

Since the summer of 2003, Woodsy's has been taking aspiring young rock musicians, grouping them with other

aspirants of near and showing the and rock a few of songs. After six sessions, the prog culminates in a c Kent Stage in whi to strut their stuff get to beam with what they got for

Every season, and its adult coun Weekend Warrior bit bigger. This students were pla bands, the most W had so far.

Please se

Drummer Brandi Walden lays down the beat on Crazy.

35

Brandi felt great about Rock School, but something was missing: her buddies Ozzie, Zach, and Isaac. Luckily, that was about to change. The guys heard all about Rock School. And they saw Brandi in the newspaper. It made them interested in getting involved.

"We were like, 'sign us up right now,'" Ozzie recalls with a laugh.

"For sure," Isaac adds. "By then, music had become the most important thing for all of us. We knew that it was time to step it up."

The timing was perfect, because it was still summer. The music store was about to start another Rock School. This time, all four teenagers signed up together.

Practicing for Rock School.

The next six weeks were very exciting. For the first time ever, Ozzie, Zach, Brandi, and Isaac were practicing together. Things clicked for them almost instantly. It was obvious that they had fantastic chemistry. It was going so well that the four of them made a huge decision. After Rock School ended, they would keep playing together. Their band had been created.

The first official Broken Heart Brigade band photo.

Of course, every band needs a name, so they started giving it a lot of thought. It *had* to be cool. It had to be a name people would remember. Zach explains what happened. "We're all tight, like family. When one of us is hurting, we're all hurting. At the time, Ozzie was going through a painful breakup with his girlfriend. One of us said how sorry we were about his broken heart."

An idea was starting to take shape. "Everyone has a broken heart at some point in their life," Zach continues. "So we decided that the four of us could represent everyone. We figured that we're like members of a broken hearts club. But the thing is, broken heart *brigade* sounds way cooler. As soon as we said it out loud, we knew it was the right name for us. From that moment forward, we were The Broken Heart Brigade."

A name can make a big difference in how people think of a band or an artist. Consider a band that was formed more than ten years ago. They called themselves Pectoralz. Ever heard of them? Probably not. Maybe they thought their name was holding them back. So, a year later, they made a switch. This time they tried out the name Starfish. Not ringing a bell yet?

You have heard of this band—but not by the name Pectoralz or Starfish. They ended up changing their name for a *third* time. By this time, they were on the road to being famous. The band is now known as Coldplay. This shows how a name—along with talent—*is* important!

In August of 2006, the final night of Rock School arrived. The Broken Heart Brigade had done well in rehearsals, but this was the real deal. Brandi already had live experience. For the three guys, however, this was their first time. They were nervous as they went on stage.

"The first couple of minutes were *very* shaky," Ozzie admits. "Because we were nervous, we were rushing and we weren't in sync."

This was understandable, but the four of them managed to get it together. By the time they began their second song, they started to relax. Ozzie's voice became strong and confident. All of a sudden, the band was in a zone. Zach and Isaac started jumping around and having a good time.

Their set included Green Day's "Holiday," and The Pink Spiders' "Little Razorblade." By the time they were finished, the crowd was on its feet. The Broken Heart Brigade was a hit. Ozzie, Zach, Brandi, and Isaac walked off the stage. Suddenly, fans rushed at them asking for autographs. People were snapping pictures and congratulating them.

"It was insane," Isaac says, shaking his head. "Here we were, having just played for the first time ever. People were treating us like rock stars! We didn't know what to think. We knew one thing for sure. This was a bigger rush than anything we had ever experienced before."

** DID YOU KNOW? ** Coldplay and Green Day both changed their band names. But they aren't the only ones. In fact, it's happened many times. Take, for instance, a rock band from England. They were originally called On a Friday. After signing their record deal, they changed their name. The inspiration for their new name was the title of an old song. The song was by the band Talking Heads, from their 1986 album True Stories. The band On a Friday became Radiohead—and went on to sell more than 25 million albums.

Chapter Five

Storyteller

She was my first kiss

I will always miss

That one time when

Her lips touched mine

Now all we have are memories

Ones we won't forget

Does she remember the first day that we met

©2006 Ozzie Thomas

"Writing a song is a very personal experience," Ozzie explains. "Sometimes an idea comes from something that's happening in my life. The inspiration for our song "On My Own" is a good example. It was based on a depressing personal situation. To tell you the truth, it's tough to talk about. So I let the song do the talking for me."

A songwriter is a storyteller who communicates through words and music. Paul Simon is a famous songwriter. He was a part of the duo Simon & Garfunkel. He once wrote a song called "The Sound of Silence." It's one of Ozzie's all-time favorites. As he says, "It grabs onto your emotions and doesn't let go."

Ozzie and Zach work out the arrangement for a new song Ozzie has written.

Every songwriter has a different approach to writing. In Ozzie's case, sometimes he starts out with the lyrics, and other times with the music. He likes to try out different chords on his guitar and sing along with them. The idea is to find a good melody to match the rhythm of the song.

Some ideas happen quickly. "On My Own" began with the chorus. Then the rest of the song just flowed out. Other ideas can take months, or even years. Ozzie talks about another song he's working on. He's been struggling with it for more than a year.

"It's a story, but I feel like I've only lived part of the story. So the song won't be complete until I have more life experience. Then I can write about it."

As for Isaac, his talent as a songwriter has grown over time. True, he's been writing lyrics for years. But it took time until he was comfortable showing his work to others. Brandi says, "Isaac was always kinda freaked out about having us use his lyrics. That's because he likes everything to be perfect."

Brandi is right about how dedicated Isaac is. Sometimes he writes a new song and the band loves it. Still, Isaac is likely to say, "I know I can make it even better." His latest song is called "Love like Lemonade." After Isaac wrote the lyrics, Ozzie came up with the music. The band has been getting very good reaction to it. They're looking forward to getting into the recording studio and recording it. Another song the band likes is a new song from Isaac. It's called "To My Dearest Dawn."

Isaac works on an idea for a new song.

Songwriters know that music relates to the way people feel about life. For example, there are millions of songs about love. Some songs are about falling in love, others are about falling out of love. There are songs about breaking up, or getting back together. And of course there are many songs about finding true love.

Love is not the only subject of songs, though. There have always been fun, strange, and even downright weird songs. Once in awhile, our country goes through big changes. These changes usually inspire songwriters. This was the case during the Civil Rights Movement of the 1960s. It was a troubled and often violent time. Hundreds of songs were written during this period.

44

A good example is the song "Ohio," by Crosby, Stills, Nash & Young. It was written about an event that took place in May of 1970. Four students who were protesting the Vietnam War were tragically killed.

On the other hand, there were also some very hopeful songs written. John Lennon wrote a famous song called "Imagine." The song talks about a world in which people live together peacefully.

More recently, our country experienced the tragic attacks of September 11, 2001. Many songs have been written about this historical event. Here are just a few of the bands and artists who have dealt with 9/11 in their music: Lifehouse, Chris Cornell, Bruce Springsteen, Evanescence, Yellowcard, and Mary J. Blige. Country star Alan Jackson also wrote a song about 9/11. He even won a Grammy Award for it. His touching song was called "Where Were You (When the World Stopped Turning)".

After 9/11, there was a musician who was inspired to create a new band. It turned out to be one of The Broken Heart Brigade's favorite bands. Gerard Way formed the band My Chemical Romance and even wrote a song about 9/11. He called it "Skylines and Turnstiles." It appeared on the band's first album, *I Brought You My Bullets, You Brought Me Your Love*.

Pride and faith: Americans come together with the singing of our national anthem.

In the fall of 2006, good things were happening for The Broken Heart Brigade. After Rock School ended, they kept practicing. They used the huge basement at Brandi's house as their practice location.

Things weren't easy at first, though. For one thing, they didn't have enough equipment to be a real band. They didn't have microphones or even mic stands. So they used an old karaoke machine instead. They taped the cord of the mic from the karaoke machine to the ceiling. That way, the mic hung down from the ceiling. "The sound quality sucked," Zach recalls with a laugh.

It wasn't a perfect situation, but nothing was going to stop this new band. They started out by choosing cover songs to perform. They practiced as much as possible, and also wrote some new songs.

One of the first covers they learned was a song by The Red Jumpsuit Apparatus. As Isaac explains, "All four of us like that band. They were going to be on the Warped tour, and we *always* go to it. So we thought it would be cool to choose one of their songs."

The song The Broken Heart Brigade chose was "Face Down." They started performing it for their friends, and at birthday and Halloween parties. They even played it at their high school talent show. Performing live was becoming their favorite thing to do. The band had been nervous that first time playing together at Rock School. They quickly got over stage fright, though. Playing in front of people was fun.

The Broken Heart Brigade was quickly turning into a good band. There are many famous bands and musicians from the state of Ohio. These include Nine Inch Nails, Bone Thugs-N-Harmony, Marilyn Manson, and Hawthorne Heights.

The Broken Heart Brigade had a long way to go, though. It was too soon to start dreaming of becoming as famous as those other musicians. So they tried to keep practicing and improving. They also looked for every chance to perform. Brandi's dad, Jack Walden, helped them out. He agreed to become the manager of the band. A manager is someone who is in charge of many things. He makes phone calls, arranges live shows, and handles other details. That way, the band can focus on practicing, writing songs, and performing.

On New Year's Eve, Ozzie, Zach, Brandi, and Isaac celebrated. They looked back on their very busy 2006. The year had been full of surprises. They realized that just 12 months earlier, everything had been different. There had been no band, no name for the band, no manager, and no live performances. The progress they had made was amazing. Things were starting to happen for The Broken Heart Brigade.

** DID YOU KNOW? ** Some artists are also respected songwriters. And sometimes their songs are recorded by other singers. R&B superstar Ne-Yo is known for his catchy songs and smooth dance moves. But most people don't realize that he is also a songwriter. His credits include Beyonce's "Irreplaceable," and Rihanna's "Unfaithful."

Chapter Six

The Studio

Most of us have heard our favorite songs too many times to count. It's natural to enjoy listening to great songs over and over. This is one reason famous bands spend so much time in the recording studio. They want their songs to be perfect.

The studio is just as important for bands that are not yet famous. The studio is where a band creates a "demo." This is short for "demonstration." It's how musicians show—or demonstrate—their talent. Bands are always trying to get music executives to listen to their demos. Sometimes that can lead to a record deal.

By the summer of 2007, The Broken Heart Brigade was ready to record their first demo. They talked it over with a friend named Aaron Shay. He was their coach from Rock School. Aaron, a talented musician and producer, had a home studio. He liked the band and their music, so he decided to produce their three-song demo.

Home studios have come a long way. You can now create CD-quality sound without spending a fortune.

Aaron explained the process to Ozzie, Zach, Brandi, and Isaac. They would spend an entire day recording just the music. Then, the following day they would record all the vocals. To complete the demo, Aaron would "mix" the three songs. This means adjusting the levels of each separate track. That way, everything blends, or "mixes" in just right.

Before The Broken Heart Brigade started recording, they had to make a decision. The band members had to choose which three songs were going to be on the demo. One of them was definitely going to be "On My Own." Song number two was an easy choice as well. They would do a cover of "Face Down," by The Red Jumpsuit Apparatus. The Broken Heart Brigade had been performing this song for almost a year. It was always a crowd favorite.

It was tough deciding on the third song. It came down to a choice between two songs. The first was "Secrets Don't Make Friends." This is a song by the band From First To Last. The second choice was "Here I stand," by the emo hardcore band Madina Lake.

The band finally decided on "Secrets Don't Make Friends." They were now ready to enter the recording studio for the first time ever. Aaron had the band members record their instruments separately. The goal was to make each track perfect. The band returned the next day and did all the vocals.

Being in the studio all day was long and tiring, especially two days in a row. It wasn't easy, but everything went smoothly. The band couldn't wait to hear the final mix.

In the meantime, cutting a demo proved to be a good experience. The band saw how cool it was to work in a recording studio. That is a career they might consider in the future.

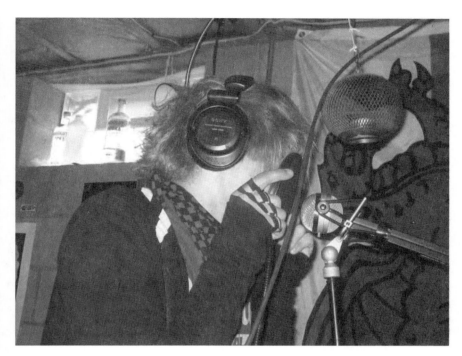

Individual performances coming together create great music. Above: Isaac. Below: Brandi.

The best thing would be if the band gets a record deal. If not, however, Ozzie, Zach, and Brandi still want to be in the music business. Who knows, they could end up working in a recording studio.

Ozzie and Zach are also interested in live shows. It takes a lot of people to put on a concert. Ozzie and Zach have talked about it. They think it might be cool to be part of a stage crew for those live shows. There are many schools that offer programs for these types of careers.

As for Isaac, he's not concerned with other careers at the moment. In his mind there's no point. He has *no* doubt that The Broken Heart Brigade is going to be a famous band. "It's okay," Brandi says with a smile. "Isaac is the youngest of all of us, only a freshman in high school. So he doesn't have to worry about college or a career just yet."

Over the next few days, Aaron was hard at work mixing the demo. He finally finished the job after putting in many long hours. He called Brandi, who jumped in the car with her dad to pick up the CD. On the way home, she sent a text to Ozzie, Zach, and Isaac. Within minutes, they all rushed over to her house. The four of them went straight downstairs to the basement. They had bought a good sound system and put it down there.

As the music poured loudly out of the speakers, the four friends sat in silence. The amazed looks on their faces told the entire story. Zach remembers saying, "Is that really *us*?" For the first time ever, they weren't simply a live band. They now had high-quality music on a CD. With this demo in hand, the entire world could hear their music. People would be able to see what The Broken Heart Brigade was all about.

The band is always hanging out together, even on top of Zach's car!

The next step was a no-brainer. They created a MySpace page. "It's been great," Brandi says. "We've gained a lot of fans through MySpace. It's been so cool getting comments and messages from people. They let us know how much they like our songs. They also say that we seem like a tight-knit band. Sometimes we hear from people we've never even met. They check out our music and find out when our next show is. We appreciate the support of our fans so much."

As the new school year got underway, a lot of things were going on for the band. First, though, it was time to party—and celebrate Brandi's 16th birthday. The Broken Heart Brigade set up tables and chairs at her house. They invited friends and family, and rocked the roof off!

Soon afterwards, the band got their first paying gig. Someone had heard about them and checked out their MySpace page. This led to an invitation to perform at a party.

Ozzie, Zach, Brandi, and Isaac arrived early to set up and do a sound check. By now, their original equipment—a karaoke machine—was long gone. It had been replaced by new mics, cords, monitors, and huge speakers.

The gig was a total success. To get hired—and paid—was amazing. The Broken Heart Brigade was worth every penny. "It was a wild show," Ozzie recalls. "At one point Isaac jumped up on the bass drum. He almost fell backwards on top of Brandi! She actually had to push him back up, but neither of them missed a beat. The audience loved it."

Holding up their very first paycheck.

As far as the demo, it was paying off as well. The band found out about a weekly request show on 88.9. It's an FM station out of Streetsboro, Ohio. They burned a copy of "On My Own" and sent it in. Someone at the station heard the song and liked it. He told the band that if people requested it, the song would be played on the air.

Ozzie, Zach, Brandi, and Isaac got the word out to their friends. Everyone started calling the station! Less than a week later, "On My Own" was on the radio for the first time ever.

This is one of the greatest thrills a musician can have. The Broken Heart Brigade will *never* forget that night. It was the very first time they heard their own song on the radio.

** DID YOU KNOW? ** There's a famous story about a demo recording. Way back in 1953, a young truck driver went to a studio. He paid $4 to record a couple of songs to give to his mom as a birthday gift. The owner of the studio happened to hear the demo. He became interested in the singer. This was a lucky twist of fate. It started the career of one of the best-selling artists of all time: Elvis Presley.

Chapter Seven

The True Essence of Music

For many people, going to a concert is the best musical experience. Think about how important it was for The Broken Heart Brigade. Brandi attended her first show at a young age. It obviously had a huge influence on her. Then she took both Ozzie and Isaac to shows that changed their lives.

When bands perform live, that's the true essence of music. "Essence" means the heart and soul of something—and live performing is definitely the heart and soul of music. The songs we enjoy in our daily lives are usually recorded in a studio. There, everything is made to sound perfect.

A live show is completely different. It's . . . well, *live*. Ozzie explains it this way: "It's about how a band plays, and how they respond to the audience. When a band plays live, that's how they *really* sound."

Before a show begins, there's a lot of excitement in the air. Like sports, it's different than watching it at home. When you're at a show, you're *part* of the action. Athletes talk about "feeding off the energy of the crowd." For musicians, it's the exact same thing.

As long as people have played music, they've performed it in front of others. There have been many famous concerts. One of them was an outdoor festival called Woodstock. It took place over four days in the summer of 1969. Hundreds of thousands of young people showed up. They camped out under the stars and cooked food on grills. They played around in the mud when it rained. It was all about having fun and doing outrageous things. Most of the time, though, it was about the music. Some of the greatest bands and artists in the world performed there.

Woodstock was truly an incredible event. To some people, it was a fitting way to end the 1960s—which was a very complicated decade. There was racial tension and an unpopular war in Vietnam. Also, tragically, two great leaders were assassinated. One was President John F. Kennedy, and the other was Dr. Martin Luther King, Jr.

Some people looked at Woodstock in a completely different way. To them, it was simply a wild celebration for young people. "I've just been to the craziest party in history!" one cheerful teenager shouted out.

Since Woodstock, there have been other successful music events. One of the largest concerts ever put on was called Live Aid. It was held in 1985. Its purpose was to raise money for starving people in the country of Ethiopia. There were concerts in America, England, and several other countries. Many famous musicians performed. Among them were U2, David Bowie, The Who, Paul McCartney, and Led Zeppelin. Hundreds of thousands of people all around the world attended the concerts. They were also on TV. More than 1.5 *billion* people watched. Talk about good ratings!

More recently, there have been a couple of great events. A concert called Live Earth took place in the summer of 2007. It featured an amazing lineup of performers. They included Kanye West, Fall Out Boy, Snow Patrol, Black Eyed Peas, Jack Johnson, Rihanna, and Chris Cornell.

In January 2009, there was another huge music celebration. It was held at the Lincoln Memorial in Washington, D.C. The concert was held to honor the inauguration of President Barack Obama. Many superstars appeared, including Beyonce, Mary J. Blige, Usher, will.i.am, Shakira, John Legend, Stevie Wonder, Bruce Springsteen, Garth Brooks, Sheryl Crow, and Bono.

The historic inauguration of President Barack Obama.

Musicians volunteer for these types of charity events. They usually don't get paid. It's simply an opportunity to give something back to the world. And, of course, it lets them do what they do best. Playing live is intense and exciting. And it's cool when it's in front of thousands of screaming fans. No matter what, though, bands love to play—even if it's just in front of a few people at a small club.

The Broken Heart Brigade feels the same way about playing live. "Performing means *everything* to us," Ozzie declares. "We want people to like our songs. But we want them to think that we're also an awesome live band. 'Emo' stands for emotion. Our emotion is all up there on stage for everybody to see."

Ozzie explains what people can expect at a Broken Heart Brigade show. "You're gonna see a little bit of everything. So you'd better be ready to have a good time! We all have a lot of energy, especially Zach and Isaac. They're always jumping up and down and running around. They've broken guitars on stage and jumped into the audience. They really get the crowd going."

Performing in front of people means always being ready. The Broken Heart Brigade has their own way of preparing for a show. Brandi, for instance, always does the same thing. Before going out on stage, she will start pacing around and loosening up. She twirls her sticks, and moves them back and forth in her fingers. She also practices air drums.

Performing live at the Kent Heritage festival.

Live performing has helped The Broken Heart Brigade grow and develop. The more they've played live, the better they've become. They've learned how to deal with unexpected things. Sometimes an amp won't work, or a cord will get tangled up. Other times a guitar string will break in the middle of a song. "We don't let anything get us or the audience down," Zach says. "When something happens, we usually just laugh about it and keep playing."

This great attitude has won them many fans. In 2007, The Broken Heart Brigade entered a "Battle of the Bands" contest. It was at a place called the Roller Hut. They put on an

excellent show and came in second place. But that's not all. The owner of the Roller Hut really liked The Broken Heart Brigade. He even booked them as the house band for some upcoming events!

It makes the band members proud that people often hire them to play. Most musicians aren't up there on stage because of money. The truth is that most bands *never* make money. When bands play in small towns, they don't get paid very much. Plus, when a band goes out on the road, there are many expenses. There are hotels, food, and transportation. Any money that *is* earned has to be divided up, sometimes among many people.

Sure, there are famous bands that make a ton of money touring. Most musicians, however, are up there for only one reason. And it's the best reason of all: the love of music—and the love of playing it live.

** DID YOU KNOW? ** To bands and their fans, live shows are the best way to connect. In September of 2006, Spin magazine listed its top 25 live bands. The Broken Heart Brigade was happy that two of their favorite bands made the list. Coming in at number 13 was My Chemical Romance. Green Day cracked the top ten, landing at number 7.

Chapter Eight

The Future Has Arrived

Hearing a lot of noise coming from Brandi's basement is pretty normal. It's what you'd expect from the practice location of a band. But on this particular day, the loud noise was a celebration. The Broken Heart Brigade had just found out something great. They had been selected to perform at a very important event. It's known as the "High School Rock-Off." This is a concert held every year at the House of Blues in Cleveland.

When the big night arrived, it felt very special. The band traveled to Cleveland in style. Their families had rented a bus so that Ozzie, Zach, Brandi, and Isaac—and a bunch of their friends—could all go together.

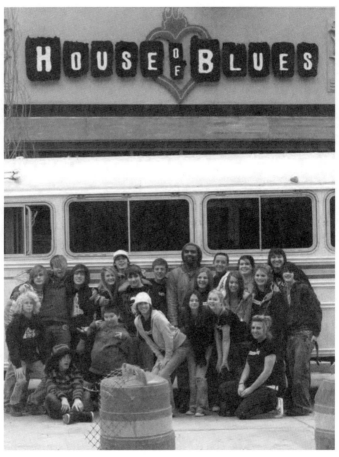

The band and friends pose for a photo in front of their party bus.

Brandi sometimes thinks back to that bus ride. It makes her remember a scene out of the film *Almost Famous*. In the movie, a teenager ends up on tour with a rock band. One of the most touching scenes takes place on a tour bus. The band and their friends start singing Elton John's hit song "Tiny Dancer." The bus ride to Cleveland felt similar. The Broken Heart Brigade, their best friend Cody Ols, and other friends were all together. They were talking, laughing, singing, and enjoying the moment.

The trip from Diamond, Ohio, took a long time because of a huge snowstorm. Luckily they had left early. Finally Ozzie, Zach, Brandi, and Isaac stepped off the bus. They started to get very excited as they approached the entrance of the House of Blues.

Walking into the House of Blues with their instruments was amazing for them. It showed exactly how far the band had come. After all, this was where Brandi had taken Isaac a few years earlier. It was the concert where they saw Simple Plan, Paramore, and Plain White T's. Now *they* were playing here!

This performance was important for many reasons. First, they would be playing in front of several music professionals. They wanted to make a good impression. If they did, it could lead to future opportunities. In addition, The Broken Heart Brigade was used to playing smaller crowds. This was about to change. The House of Blues holds over 1,000 people.

Backstage, Ozzie talked to Daryl, the stage manager. He told Ozzie that he would be calling for the band in about 20 minutes. Daryl's bright purple cap said "HOUSE OF BLUES" in bold capital letters.

Zach and Isaac relax backstage before showtime at the House of Blues.

As Ozzie, Zach, Brandi, and Isaac sat backstage and waited, they realized something. They realized that this opportunity could be very important for their future. And this is something they care about very much. Maybe in the back of their minds was the song "The Future Has Arrived." It's a song by one of their favorite bands, The All-American Rejects.

Thinking about the future of the band, Ozzie and Zach have made a huge decision. They will both be graduating soon from high school. They realize they have a good thing going with The Broken Heart Brigade. So both of them will be going to Kent State University. It's less than 25 miles away from Diamond. In other words, they're sticking close to home. This means the band will continue on for a long time.

Brandi and Isaac are very happy about this. In fact, Brandi will be in the same position in less than a year. Right now she's only a junior. She would love to travel outside of Ohio one day. She thinks it would be cool to live in a big city like New York or Los Angeles. Still, the band is her number one priority. So she's planning on attending Kent State also.

There's no way to know where The Broken Heart Brigade will end up. Ozzie, Zach, Brandi, and Isaac dream of "making it." But think about something. They have *already* made it. How lucky are they to have discovered their love of playing music? Sure, they want a record deal and the chance to make a lot of money. But the joy of having music in their lives means more to them than anything else.

This is something music fans can relate to. Think of how different the world would be without music. How strange would it be to watch a TV show if there were no sound effects? How about watching a scary movie without the creepy music that lets us know something is about to happen? Of course, you can't forget video games. It's hard to imagine playing a video game without music.

Music isn't simply entertainment. It goes to the very heart of who we are as people. We all listen to music. This is why we appreciate the artists who create it.

One day The Broken Heart Brigade may be famous. They may be like My Chemical Romance, or one of the other bands they admire. But they're already doing many of the same things as those bands. They work on new songs, record music, and perform live. So it's not about where Ozzie, Zach, Brandi, and Isaac will be tomorrow . . . it's about where they are and what they're doing right now. The future *has* arrived.

This photo was snapped moments before The Broken Heart Brigade took the stage for the Rock-Off.

The audience at the House of Blues in Cleveland can get very loud. Tonight was no different. Even from backstage, it was obvious that the crowd was amped up. 20 minutes passed quickly. Suddenly, Daryl was standing right in front of Ozzie, Zach, Brandi, and Isaac. He straightened his bright purple "HOUSE OF BLUES" cap. Then he motioned for them to follow him. They all walked to the area behind the stage. "You're on," Daryl screamed over the sound of the crowd. "Get ready, they're gonna introduce you. I'll open the curtain in one minute."

The band jumped onto the stage, behind a giant curtain. All of a sudden, they heard themselves being introduced. The crowd cheered as the curtain opened. There were hundreds of fans stamping their feet and clapping. Many people in the crowd had heard about The Broken Heart Brigade. They were eager to see them perform.

Brandi tapped her drumsticks four times and looked over at Ozzie. With a smile, he played the opening notes of "On My Own." Then the rest of the band joined in. Isaac started thumping the heavy notes of his bass. Zach jumped high in the air as he struck the power chords of the verse. Together they created a wall of sound. It was very powerful. It was the band doing what they do best.

One time I met this girl
Changed my whole world
We fell for each other
And it all worked out
'Til one day we started
A fight over nothing at all
We tried to make things work
Then we fell into a doubt

As soon as Ozzie sang the opening lines, every seat in the place was empty . . . because everyone stood up. Some teenagers even rushed the stage. They wanted to watch up close

Brandi, and Isaac understand quite well. It's the way *they* feel when they go to see a band they love. It's something only a true music fan can appreciate. Once you've had that experience, it stays with you forever.

For The Broken Heart Brigade, it's all about the music. That's all it's ever been about. There's nothing Ozzie, Zach, Brandi, and Isaac enjoy more than being in front of people— playing music live. And when they're not doing that, they're likely to be at a concert—watching live music.

When you get right down to it, they *live* music.

www.myspace.com/thebrokenheartbrigade